Family Gathering

Family Gathering

p o e m s

Fred Chappell

Louisiana State University Press   Baton Rouge   MM

Manufactured in the United States of America
First printing
09 08 07 06 05 04 03 02 01 00
5 4 3 2 1

Designer: Barbara Neely Bourgoyne
Typeface: Centaur and Minion
Printer and Binder: Thomson-Shore, Inc.

Library of Congress Cataloging-in-Publication Data

Chappell, Fred, 1936–
    Family gathering / Fred Chappell
       p. cm.
    ISBN 0-8071-2625-X (cloth : alk. paper) — ISBN 0-8071-2626-8 (pbk. : alk. paper)
    1. Family—Poetry. I. Title.

PS3553.H298 F35 2000
811'.54—dc21

                                                                              00-040561

The author wishes to thank the editors of the following journals in which
some of these poems were previously published, often in different forms:
Brightleaf, The Review, White Pelican Review, and *Victoria Press 2000.*

To my ancient mistress
the University of North Carolina, Greensboro

Contents

Family Gathering

Elizabeth Retreats

Seated, they become one with their chairs,
And when they stand the ceiling is too low;
The histories that call them to converse
Are as obscure as the Carthaginian wars
And elegiac as this evening's afterglow.

Among them roams Elizabeth, age eight,
Priss-proud in her finery and bored
Bored bored. Grown-ups do nothing always but sit
And talk, and what do they ever talk about?
—Not of Elizabeth a single word.

Even her daddy brushes her aside
And discomposes into self-important wrinkles
When he leans forward, nervous, dissatisfied,
Talking heatedly, wagging his head
At the freckled knuckles of half-drunken uncles.

Are you Elizabeth if no one says?
Nor compliments your dress with its blue sash,
Remarks your brilliant patent leather shoes?
They let you wander and listen all you please,
But pay you no more mind than cigar ash.

The kitchen aunts and great-aunts boil and bake,
Gossip of diets, hysterectomies,
Disasters, cures, deep woe and long heartache,
As if they traded recipes for cake
Or retold the plots of soapy TV shows.

The other older children will not engage,
The young are babies or insufferably dumb;
No one here is of a proper age
To understand Elizabeth at this stage
When all that's good is past or yet to come.

Out to the porch she goes, where the starless night
Presses against the sagging rusty screens
Its breathing flank. The yellow ceiling light
Attracts a fairy moth whose zigzag flight
Throws shadow-scuttle on the window panes.

The inside of the house seems far away
With all its clutter, chatter, whiskey breath
And coffee. Very well—better to stay
Alone. Solitary, she can play
Her favorite role: the true Elizabeth.

She cuts the light, begins to pirouette,
Measuring a tune that pours her mind
Full of itself, a lilting minuet
That spins her ever faster than her feet.
Elizabeth is dancing, dancing blind,

Inside the porch inside a night so black
That it could swallow house and family
Like irritated Godzilla run amok.
Only this ritual can keep the monster back;
Her plaintive song must charm the enemy.

Uncle Einar

When Uncle Einar smokes his big cigar,
His pink cheeks glow, his blue eyes glaze;
An expensive aromatic haze
Hallows the shining of his cranium;
His nose smolders like a red geranium.
His eyes roll heavenward where cherubim
Gambol the dove-gray smoke that pours from him,
And with a sound like forcing the Pearly Gates,
He opens his golden mouth and pontificates
To all his dim kinfolk less fortunate
Than he with stocks and bonds and real estate.
They know they're in the presence of a star
When Uncle Einar smokes his big cigar.

When Uncle Einar drives his Cadillac car
He rolls the window down so his cigar
Can have some elbow room and freshen up
For miles and miles around the drab landscape
That heretofore has had to be content
With raw fresh air wholly lacking the scent
Of Havana tobacco that smells like yellow roses
As it fumes beneath Uncle Einar's loud proboscis.
He rolls along at eighty miles an hour,
His tape deck blaring Sinatra at full power
Unless Aunt Wilma has accompanied
Her burnished husband for a Sunday ride;
For she insists on hymn tunes cranked up loud
To remind them both they owe it all to God.
You know you've seen the streaking of a star
When Uncle Einar drives his Cadillac car.

When Uncle Einar lets his intellect soar,
His groundling kinfolk sit around and stare
As he sucks upon his velvety cigar
And expatiates upon his Cadillac car.

Such sterling precepts from his wisdom pour
That every bromide glows like cinnabar
As he explains the profits of peace and war,
The economies of nations near and far,
And how to gain the peso, drachma, kroner, yen, dinar,
By knowing who you know and being who you are.
Yet livid thunderstorms around him roar
When he contemplates the multitudinous poor
Who seem to lack the slightest instinct for
Keeping the ravenous wolf outside their door.
But lest they spoil the pleasure of this hour,
Uncle Einar thrusts such thoughts afar
And pours a cognac from a Baccarat jar.
The twinkling brightness of a double star:
That's Uncle Einar and his vast cigar.

Uncle John

One may say of Uncle John he's *there*,
But not that "there" is changed by this cool fact.
He's not invisible, the way that air
And metaphysics are. He'll speak and act,
As other people do, and yet he's seen
But hardly noticed, like a nondescript
Monument amid excited children
Playing in the park at green twilight.

The thought has been advanced that Uncle John
Should not be counted with the human race
But rather as a separate phenomenon,
An extensive quality of physical space
Like *length* and *width* and *depth,* a whole dimension
Unto himself unmarked. —Contrariwise,
Some claim such blandness is his sly intention,
That he's perfected a helluva good disguise.

If you believe in spooks, then Uncle John
May fit your definition—unless you find
That he's too incorporeal for one,
Making such slight impression on the mind
That he'd be snubbed by any proper ghost.
And yet I've wondered if that's not his plan:
In mortal flesh he lives as a specter lost
So when he dies he'll come back as a man.

Genealogist

Cousin Elmer tends the family tree,
Shaping it to topiary rare
And strange as he trims a little here and there
And lops some ugly branches drastically.

It's crystal clear to him that we're descended
From renownèd figures of a heroic time,
Our annals innocent of any crime.
His usual skepticism is suspended

When he turns his eye upon our heritage.
Not that he means to practice a deception,
He only has an immaculate conception
Of what we must have been in a former age.

But look at us. Isn't the evidence plain
That we are nothing special, never were?
Our history is ordinary and bare,
Our biographies boring as eight days of rain.

It's improbable even to suppose
He'd ever find a drop of noble blood,
Tracing roots of a dull ignoble wood.
The jack pine never did put forth a rose.

The Calculator

In the babbling study Uncle Nahum takes
A shadowed seat in a nameless corner where
He can observe, drawing no least stare
From the gossipy others. His silence never breaks.

He drinks no coffee, whiskey, cola, tea;
He eats no cherry cobbler or mince pie;
He wears a nondescript suit, a boring tie,
An image of alert serenity.

He studies his kinfolk closely and could say
More names than they remember. He compares
Their ages to his own ninety-six years.
Who will be the next to pass away?

He numbers it an article of faith
There will be fewer at next year's gathering;
The seasons trundle and evermore they bring
Each of us closer to the gates of death—

Except for Uncle Nahum who shows no clue
He's watched a century's winters come and go,
Enshrouding several dozen with featureless snow.

You shiver just a little when he looks at you.

Aunt Wilma Describes Her Many Charms

This cute monkey's made of platinum
With itsy-bitsy rubies for his eyes;
Your Uncle Einar did something truly dumb,
So little "Cutie Monkey" was my prize.
Every charm upon this bracelet chain
Tells the tale of how it came my way.
Einar thinks he's quite the sexy man,
And when I catch him, then I make him pay.

"Chase the floozies from here to Kingdom Come,
Make them promises and tell them lies,"
I said, "but sooner or later you'll crawl home—
And I'll be waiting with a big surprise.
You may imagine you've endured some pain
And that you've suffered many a doleful day,
But chop this thought into your marble brain:
Every time I catch you, you will pay."

This little donkey's from Jerusalem,
Where he tried a Swedish tourist on for size;
In Liverpool he had another whim
For which he paid with darling white jade mice.
I'd best not tell you what he did in Spain—
Einar's a dog and dogs will have their day—
But the pain in Spain well nigh drove him insane
Because I caught him and he had to pay.

Your Uncle Einar and his shiny dome
Are more attractive than you realize
To certain types a little past their bloom;
His every misstep swells my menageries
With cunning little animals that shine
And jingle on my bracelet display,
Adding music to my old refrain:
Any time I catch you, you will pay.

There was an escapade in Amsterdam
Resulting in these charming ivory dice;
In Montreal he nearly sealed his doom:
This snowflake set with diamonds met my price.
—You think I'm mercenary, don't you, Fran?
Well, listen carefully, girl, to what I say:
A woman my age must do all she can
To nab her husband and to make him pay.

For youth's as fleeting as the lacy foam
That fringes sea waves under typhoon skies,
Delicate as webwork in a disused room
Where winter spiders dream of summer flies.
And what is left for us when youth is gone,
When our charms like snowdrops melt away?
A husband possesses a flea's attention span—
So when he wanders you must make him pay.

The Clencher

You start to enlighten Uncle Brit
About your views on the economy.
You start—and there's the end of it.
He cuts you off before you say
Two sentences and lets you know
He knows already what you think
And what you think is pretty dumb.
He wouldn't flush it down the sink,
He's too polite for that, though some
Of his acquaintance wouldn't be—
They'd trash your notions mercilessly.

It's no use trying to remonstrate;
He shouts you down in tones so loud
The noise is like a ton of freight
Tumbling off a mountainside.
Every dialogue is a combat
That he must win at any cost;
He'd argue with a sleeping wombat
Or with a whitewashed hitching post.
When he feels his argument
Is weak he's more aggressive still;
His tense resolve grows hard as flint
To bend his opponent to his will.
When proven wrong he's satisfied
That victory still is on his side.

For even when he's wrong he's right;
You probably misunderstood
The question. Examine it in the light
Of serene reason, as he would;
You'll come to different conclusions.
He's thought it out and seen quite through

All the troublesome confusions
That facts and figures add to the view.

Let's have no pointless shedding of blood.
You know you're in the wrong, don't you?

Aunt Bettie, Resigned

Our pleasures ashes, the bills are falling due;
       We stumble through a blizzard of arrears.
I'm growing older. Thank God, so are you.

The orchid-brilliant evenings now are few
       And far between. We bore ourselves to tears.
Our pleasures ashes, the bills are falling due.

Do you recall the spats about each new
       Affair we each suspected? Now neither cares.
I'm growing older. Thank God, so are you.

Somewhere a waltz is playing in a blue
       Ballroom, couples dancing, brash young dears.
Our pleasures ashes, the bills are falling due,

We've failed at last to make the untrue true
       And now the truth, with all its horror, nears.
I'm growing older. Thank God, so are you.

We had our time, then something slid askew.
       You kissed my mouth; you promised carefree years.
Our pleasures ashes, the bills are falling due,
And I've grown older, thank God. So have you.

The Album

Grandma Settle turns the pages slowly,
Murmuring to Emily and Tom.
"This picture," she explains, "shows Uncle Crowley
When he returned from soldiering in Siam.
He never was quite the same after his stretch
In the Orient. He contracted a disease
That undermined his health and cured his itch
To roam. He never again shipped overseas."

The children nod. Her hand upon the pages,
Time-stippled, wrinkled, pausing at each face,
Seems to belong as much to former ages
As do these photographs of an alien race
That must have flourished when the world was new
And Moses and Jesus shared a desert tent,
Blue-eyed Columbus sailed the ocean blue,
And dinosaurs stamped the steamy continent.

"Oh, look!" she exclaims. "Isn't this hat silly?
But people used to dress like this, you know.
Here's Aunt Margaret with Uncle Billy
Beside their Ford all covered up with snow;
Uncle Billy was your Cousin Harold's dad.
Here's Baby Austin who died when he was ten:
His mother's heart was broken; her mind went bad;
She never spoke to a living soul again."

The heavy pages turn, the children look
Forward in time. Whose picture will they see,
Whose story hear, as Grandma makes the book
Whisper with legend? She travels the other way,
Backward through the flat vivid decades,
To years before she and Grandpa were wed,
Before the wars arrived, and all the lads
Were handsome, tall, and brave, and none was dead.

Cousin Ellie

We remember Ellie when
She was a blue-eyed girl of ten.
Her hair was silver, her laugh was wild,
Her heart wiser than the heart of a child.

Yet now we wish we could erase
The image of that childhood face.
That face is changed, and changed her mind
By careless days that lie behind.

Alas, that we remember when
She was a glad-eyed girl of ten.
Thirty years have passed since then;
Thirty years and thirty men.

Scorekeeper

Cousin Lola charts her paramours
On a performance scale from One to Ten
And then announces publicly the scores.
She's sweet and cheerful and, in her way, refined,
And maybe that's why no one seems to mind—
    Except, of course, the Zero men.

Cousin Lilias

Within a shadow dark as murmurs, wise
As midnight, Cousin Lilias slides, footfalls
Noiseless as spiders' thought. Her amber eyes
Are slow and watchful, as if she hunts for prey.
She seems to move in time to a bell that tolls
Beyond the careful measures of night and day,
Her mind a prospect of indifferent skies.

No one talks with her. The family
Falls quiet when at last her velvet presence
Is noticed in the room. What did she see?
What does she know? She is the palpable essence
Of something they cannot name, cool mystery
From otherwhere, black skirt and leotard.
She sets off with mascara-ebony
Those eyes that with a blink can go quartz-hard.

Finding herself detected, she sidles through
The doorway, depositing a silence within
The room that is not easily dispelled.
No one wants to be the first to say
A word, no one even coughs. Quelled
Like suspects being arraigned, they glumly scan
The carpet, as if seeking a hopeful clue.

Sooner shall pert scientists unravel
The riddle of existence than these shall know
Cousin Lilias's secret. Evil
And Good shall be as one; the Tower of Babel
Shall rise once more; Noah from Ararat
Set sail; volcanoes erupt vanilla snow . . .
For she is the puppet of her Alter Ego,
That ominous brilliant schemer, Grimoire, her cat.

Cousin Marjorie

Oh when she's there she's so immensely there
No color but her own, no voice but hers,
No other nature can advance itself;
She is the noontime that absorbs the day-moon.

Large in every sense, rich, overblown,
Rose that droops from surfeit of itself;
Bright flowing dresses brave as carnival bunting:
All Marjorie's grand Everything is here.

The dimpled hands, the sensual smile, the stare
That takes you in as warmly as a perfume,
All sympathy and calm attentiveness:
So much herself it seems she has no self

But only Presence that if taken away
Would cause such lessening of the sense of place
You'd think the room was now no more itself
But only a diminished facsimile:

A room wherein a chamber symphony
Played Schubert for an hour and then removed,
The chairs left emptier than before they came.
So much herself she is wild Selflessness,

Has no more concept of a Marjorie
Than has a waterfall, a sunbaked stone,
The dew-strung spider web, the snuffling spaniel,
The rain-wet sweet gum spread-armed in City Park.

Adventures in Perception

1

Uncle Jack
Is rather fat
But thinks he's skin and bone.

Aunt Jill is thin
As her bright hatpin
But thinks she weighs a ton.

2

Uncle Nash knows he's an idiot
But he doesn't give a shidiot.

3

Aunt Beth and Uncle Philip disagree
And yet agree.
Misunderstanding keeps their marriage fit,
Unsplit
By jealous quarrels, for each secretly
And all alone
Believes that one of them has married down.
She thinks it's she.
He he.

Collusion

Less than he seems is the buzz on Cousin Brice.
                    No one denies that he's as nice
As any fellow you might care to meet,
Yet you can never put your finger on
Any beneficence that he has done;
                    You only think of him as "sweet."

Maybe it's his smile, so absentminded
There's surely nothing ulterior behind it;
Maybe it's his cheerful social grace,
                    An easygoing deference
That never engages with, therefore wins
Over any situation he may face.

For you create your cousin as you chat,
Emitting signals you're unconscious of
That he, like a lady trying on a glove,
Snugly receives, begins to tug to fit,
Shaping an image that he hopes you'll love.

So if he's less a person than a conduit,
All the fault is not with Cousin Brice.
He only wants to put you at your ease,
                    Always attempting to intuit
If any characteristic does not please:
You made him once; you can make him twice.

                    Thrice.

The Rubaiyat of Uncle Hobart

1

Come, let us tipple while the diva Moon
Warbles her seductive "Clair de Lune,"
   Silencing the Nightingale and Owl
To keep close Harmony with my wry Bassoon!

2

Midway in this life I paused to think
What Way to choose before me, on that Brink
   Of Time whereafter few turn back, then heard
A pleasant Voice exhorting me to drink

3

While yet the Sun against the Mountain Side
Cast all the glowing Treasure of his Pride
   And with a careless Prodigality
The Night and all its spear-sharp Stars defied.

4

Let them write on their monkish Vellum what
For Aeons they have posted: *Thou shalt not.*
   In their dim Cells they hear the gray Dust rustle;
The Mocking Bird enthralls my Garden Plot.

5

Four Wives I wed that now beneath the Sod
Are mercifully transformed to Clay and Clod.
   The Rose that blooms upon their neighbor Graves
I praise, a *Silent* Glory of our God.

6

Passion passes, but its golden Clime
Warms the Spirit for a certain Time;
      The Memory of that Season warms me still,
As does this present Glass of Gin and Lime.

7

I read World History with careful Eyes
To learn the Nations and their Destinies,
      Discovering that All go to inherit
The selfsame Soil their Heroes fertilize.

8

To Poetry then I turned, hoping anew
To hear some Echo of the immortally True.
      "Seize Present Time, and let the Future go":
The old sad Tune that I already knew.

9

Suppose that perfect into this World we came,
Our Souls angelic and our Minds the same,
      What were we then, or what should ever be?
Faceless Counters in an Idiot's Game.

10

Myself I did protect when anyone
Threatened my Person with a Blade or Gun,
      But now with Cup and Flagon defend against
An ancient, cackling, rheum-eyed, toothless Crone.

11

So let us stroll into a friendly Bar
And raise to passing Time a cheerful Jar,
      Although swift Time can take no Heed of us,
And is not ours either to mend or mar.

12

Should ever Barkeep fail to fill my Glass
With Beaujolais that aids blue Hours to pass,
      Demanding Coin that I do not possess,
I'm just the Man to kick his worthless Ass.

Nothing in Excess

"We must refine our senses," Uncle Wallace said,
        "Otherwise existence
      Overwhelms us with a brute insistence
      On the thingness of things, whatness of what.
      Distinguish forty variant shades of red:
Pearl-pink from blush, scarlet from cerise,
        Bland lukewarms from hots,
Tepids from cools—and do so with an offhand ease."

Uncle Wally continued, as was ever his wont:
        "Not as an idle pastime
      That one engages whenever one has time
      And then puts by again as occasion suits,
      But as a noble accomplishment to flaunt
      Before one's unadept acquaintances
        Like a mastery of flutes,
Theorbos, galliards, and other necessities.

"If you can name the spot a certain wild thyme grows
        And then recognize
      Its character without the aid of eyes
      Or tongue, you shall have made a sound beginning.
      Other smells will cultivate a nose
      Knowledgeable of faint subtleties
        No other kind of training
Acquires, though you may study for scented centuries."

He twirled his wine stem deftly, then commenced again:
        "The intimacy of touch
      May exercise awareness overmuch
      Unless you learn to regulate the need
      Your organism has even for pain;
      It hankers after sensations of every kind
        With what amounts to greed
And for that reason must be sternly disciplined.

"To course a comely woman's skin with fingertip,
                    Thus being able to know
          Whether by candlelight her hair will show
          As blond or strawberry or deep brunette
          As you trace along her jawline, neck, and lip
          With your eyes closed requires an expertise
                    Difficult to get
In a world of crass excess and blunt stupidities."

He held his glass against the light and gazed into
                    His drop of pale champagne:
          "We learn the *terroir* differences between
          Neighboring vineyards in the Bordeaux region
          And taste the tints in a rosé of Anjou—
          And yet within a single glass of wine
                    Distinctions are as legion
As those among the many grapes upon one vine.

"Our faculty of hearing should be purified.
                    One mustn't discover 'staccato'
          Merely but a thousand shapes of pizzicato;
          The varying timbres of a fermata note
          Will seem, upon close listening, to glide
          Into one another like veil on veil
                    Lifted lightly afloat;
One lonely tone implies a pentatonic scale.

"Truly to distinguish colors one must first see light
                    Not as a medium
          Which the individual pigments strum
          With each its own peculiar vibration,
          But as a physical entity, both bright
          And dark at once, that interpenetrates,
                    According to situation,
The objects that it touches and with which it mates."

Then Uncle Wallace inhaled his empty champagne glass
                    As appreciatively

As if it held a precious rarity
Rather than some remnant molecules
Of Perignon now sipped off, alas.
He pursed his lips and gave a dainty kiss,
　　　Saluting the misled fools
Who do not hoard but sell such wizard stuff as this.

"And love, ah yes, love—," he whispered with a sigh.
　　　　　"It's not a gross machine
That roars foul smoke and gobbles gasoline;
The music it requires is never rock
And roll but a gossamer strain of melody
Murmured in his calmest dulcet style
　　　By Philip Emmanuel Bach
For oboe, bassoon, three violins, French horn, and viol.

"Sometime you have observed a pair of dragonflies
　　　　　In process of mating,
Lucent above the water, hesitating
In air the brightest of fleeting instants before
They skim away, as if this enterprise
Of love were too intense to occupy
　　　The whole of their beings more:
They practice the invaluable art of love on the fly.

"Such custom seems to me an ideal consummation:
　　　　　An airborne sunny taste
Of Eros, swiftly enjoyed, though without haste,
Anxiety, or afterthought. Yet all
One's incandescent and consuming passion
Discovered, performed, fordone without regret,
　　　Perhaps without recall . . .
Then to uncouple, unencumbered and separate."

He circled the thin flute rim with a practiced finger,
　　　　　Making the crystal ring
Like a taut-drawn filament of silver string
And listened to the plaintive note so close

It seemed that he might be content to linger
With its evanishment for hour on hour
As one might watch a rose
At twilight let its petals fall in a slow shower.

"Life is too short for hurry, too powerful for force
Of will, rage of desire;
It's not a fortress to be taken by fire
Or catapult or cannon. It is perfume
Or tinted mist or shadow, endless source
Of intimations that will never reveal,
This side of the tomb,
Some single enormous truth that we would hail the Real.

"Let us therefore pour another lively swallow
Of wine that brightens the eye,
Brightens the mind as clear as a windswept sky
And cheers a spirit that philosophy
Burdens with doubt or tramples to a wallow
Of gray despair, even while the sun
Is prating steadily
Horizon to horizon its carefree orison.

"It is not wise to plunder with spendthrift rapine
Our time that is so brief
It seems but a season's shedding of a leaf
That lately wore a vivid virile green
But now portends the ending of the year.
Savor life. Do not become besotted."

Never did we hear
Such praise of moderation from a man so potted.

Packrat

Cousin Reeves
Saves lengths of string
For he believes
That everything
Will prove useful
When least expected.
His house is full
Of ruck collected,
Awaiting the hour
When the bent and rusted,
The mold-encrusted,
Will regain their power
And be resurrected
To their former glory.

That's his whole story.

Morris

The chair she sat in with an earnest groan
Was lumpy, frumpy, boggy, saggy, butt
Sprung and dingy, weary to the bone
And older than the pleasures of King Tut.

Where it came from no one now recalled;
It was so long a part of Family
Nobody noticed how it had grown bald
And spavined, unsteady as Uncle McGhee.

Aunt Edna would sit there like she owned the place,
And yet she seemed a property of the chair,
As beauty is a property of grace,
Right angles the properties of a square.

Now Aunt Edna's gone. The chair remains,
With drowsy Audrey nestled in its warm
Complacent cushions with their ancient stains
And mends and redolent maternal charm.

It comforts her as it has comforted
Two generations of kin and eight of cats.
No longer proud, its noblest glories fled,
It humbly supports purses, kerchiefs, hats.

The Long View

Uncle Abner studies history
And takes a slow, considered view of things.
The latest scandals of the President,
The Congress, Senate, and the Chiefs of Staff
Haven't reached him yet. He ponders still
Whether Polk's election was legitimate,
Whom to blame in the Hamilton-Burr affair,
And if we should get into World War II.

His sentences are works of majesty:
They open coolly glowing like predawn light
And close like velvet curtains coming down
Upon a scene of antique rituals
With personages who declaim in stately periods
Ideas so solemn they cast reverend shadows.
His tone of voice, his precisely measured demeanor
Project such dark regret, such deep world-sorrow
You feel a little pity for all he knows.
What he knows has not brought happiness,
Only the peace a desert may afford.

Your voice grows louder as you talk to him,
As if the distance widened between you both,
He moveless in one spot, you carried away
Downstream in time, gesticulating, shouting,
Alarmed by a force you never knew before.
He sees you there—you're certain that he sees you,
Watches you diminish, smaller and dimmer
As you become a part of history,
A mite, a mote, a molecule, an atom
Indistinguishable from the other atoms.
You feel your spirit gutter, your name drain from you,
All hope extinguish of being even a footnote.

True Believer

Uncle Zack believes that we will thrive
   By doing everything the Bible says.
Thou shalt not suffer a witch to live.

   Whatever happened to Aunt Inez?

Nonbeliever

But Cousin Terry thinks that Holy Writ
   Holds no authority, not a whit,
Although, to score a point, he'll quote a bit.

   Oh, what a filthy hypocrite!

Glad Hand

Two hundred twenty-five
Pounds of bonhomie,
Uncle Jake's all jive
And boundless jollity.
He always knows your name,
Never forgets a face;
He hails you just the same,
Though fifteen years may pass.
He loves to shake your hand
And clap you on the shoulder,
To tell you that he's found
You don't look one day older.

And then the both of you
Strike an expectant pose,
Those it's obvious that he too
Has said everything he knows.
You repeat you're feeling well
While searching for swift egress
From the hollow grinning hell
Of his desperate friendliness.
But you cannot get away;
He recalls a witticism
He hopes will make you stay
Till he snares another victim.

The joke falls flat. His smile
Becomes a sick grimace
That lets you know his soul
Feels its shabby disgrace.
He turns upon his heel
And leaves you standing there,
Forcing you to face
Your own guilty despair.

Secretless

Cousin Vance you know instinctively
Has no secrets. Open as a plain
In Kansas, guileless as a terrapin,
Straightforward, candid to the nth degree
He tells you anything you'd like—and more.

Is this what makes him such a thumping bore?

Wallflower

Cousin Jill is shy
"Modest to a fault."
She always lingers by
The edges of a crowd;
Her evening's fairly spoilt
If she's forced to talk aloud.
But it's not timidity—
She fancies that everyone
Knows what she has done.

Mistaken Premise

Cousin Willoughby owns an antique shop
And dreams of days when little boys
Were thought quite suitable erotic toys
For older men. Those noble centuries
Gave birth, he claims, to art that never dies.
To grand achievements in philosophy,
Science, politics, geometry;
Succeeding eras yield a scrawny crop.

Cousin Burke detests the swishy sight
Of Willoughby. "The family disgrace,"
He calls the fellow, though never to his face;
He tries to keep his ire under control,
But still his head will wag, his eyes will roll
As Willoughby imparts Gay History
To uncles listening not quite comfortably
And striving mightily to be polite.

"Plato, Tchaikovsky, Michelangelo—"
Willoughby names them off with sweet aplomb—
"And all the others whose genius strikes us dumb:
They worked for the common good of humankind
And left for us such monuments of the mind
That we owe them a debt of gratitude
We never could repay, try as we would."
He shuts his eyes, his hands flit to and fro.

Burke he thinks the loutiest on the globe:
My dumbass cousin, what could he ever know
Of Diaghilev, Nijinsky, Jean Cocteau?
He has no sense of art or literature;
He's quite convinced that it's all horse manure.
He lives his life as if it's his design
To be the model of a philistine,
A jerk, a clod, a redneck homophobe.

But Willoughby has got things partly wrong.
It's true his cousin doesn't care for art,
And yet he's got a wild romantic heart
And by his passions is all too thoroughly swayed.
It's only that bluff Burke prefers rough trade;
It's farmers, boxers, bus and taxi drivers,
Guys who work the docksides on the rivers,
And scarfaced sailors he goes down among.

Hubert

Even sniveling's an art,
If you learn how and practice hard.
Cousin Hubert knows it pat:
He never sits before you sit,
He never speaks before you speak
(And then you'd swear he never spoke),
Never precedes you through a door;
He lives in order to defer,

If we can call it living. Why
Does he slouch in that hangdog way?
His mother, "the Little General,"
Approves his every small detail,
Haircut, shoes, and suit and tie,
His reading list, his fiancée.
"Hubert, stand up straight!" she orders,
Thus inspiring several murders
Of a wonderfully grisly kind
In Hubert's scarlet, viscous mind.
"Yes mam," he says, in a tone so glum
It's bound to mean, *You've sealed your doom.*

Aunt Alicia and the Facts of the Case

She loves to gossip, Aunt Alicia does;
The problem is, her memory's all fuzz,
And so she can't attach the proper name
To the proper personage and must defame
At random, the way a dandelion throws
Its seeds to sail the wind wherever it blows.
Did Cousin Danny rob a jewelry store
Or did he lately move to Labrador?
Was Cousin Doris married in Detroit
Or was she mangled by an ocelot?

It's quite a jolt sometimes. You hear it said
Three members of your family are dead
And think, *We dwindle to a precious few*—
Then see them Sunday sitting in their pew.
Scandal she stores in opulent supply;
At every word two reputations die;
A third escapes, but that's the very one
She should have pinned her naughty story on.
Her sources place her accuracy past doubt,
She claims. Why are you startled to find out
Your younger sister's run off with an Eskimo?
It must be true, she says—*you* told her so.

Yet you forgive her bumbling because she
Confers a fickle immortality.
For a while you're dead, and then you rise,
Resurrected by her memories
That flicker dim then brighten up again
The way an April day shifts sun and rain. . . .
Once she declared, with dark eyes sad and round,
That she herself was dead and underground.

Aunt Lavinia Strikes

Aunt Wilma's fabled spoon bread sits
Beside Aunt Martha's perennial grits;
Here Sissie's chicken à la king
Companions Darla's Jell-O ring,
While Cousin Willoughby has brought in
A gay attempt at *haute cuisine,*
And next—the terror of the soul:
Aunt Lavinia's casserole.

The years come round and, as they do,
Cousin Barney's Irish stew
Will return again somehow
To take an undeserving bow,
Along with Mother Elsie's bread,
A stone to commemorate the dead,
Like the victims we enroll
Under "Aunt Lavinia's Casserole."

Uncle Zeph asks blessing on
The peach preserves and crisp cornpone
Aunt Matilda so tediously made,
And the zucchini marmalade
Brought by crazy Uncle McGhee
He includes democratically;
But his blessing is not whole—
It omits the casserole.

The fumes it breathes are strong enough
To set the smoke detectors off;
The radon gauge screams into red,
The Geiger counters go stark mad.
The laws of physics confirm our fears—
A half-life of four billion years:
For mankind's future we *must* control
Aunt Lavinia's casserole;

Or else it's what our family
Will bequeath to all eternity:
An angry, evil, black morass
Slowly approaching critical mass.
Ages will roll, constellations change,
Gemini into Virgo range,
And then the system from pole to pole
Will collapse into the Casserole.

Traddutore, Traditore

Uncle Barber's tangled tongue
    Turns his words to mush;
Vowel, consonant, diphthong
    Thicken into slush.

We know that he's intelligent;
    The expressions of his face
Give us a hint, more than a hint,
    Dementia's not the case.

Aunt Hannah interprets his every word,
    Yet as we follow along
Some things she says are so absurd
    She must have got them wrong.

We cannot avoid a dark suspicion:
    Isn't there more than a tinge
In her tone of caustic, mocking derision?

    That would be her perfect revenge.

The Jitters

Cousin Deddle won't meet your gaze,
Nor will he occupy one place
For more than a fiddly moment or so.
His fit is on him; he must go
Forward and backward everywhere,
Butterfly tumbling turbulent air.

He has no purpose you can discern;
He isn't curious to learn,
He isn't anxious you should hear
Any message he might bear.
A finger drummer, a pacer, a wriggler,
A shrugger, a shuffler, a nervous giggler,
He twiddles his buttons and his buckles,
Scratches his crotch and cracks his knuckles;
He rattles loudly his saucer and cup.

Whatever he fears is catching up.

The Utter Failure

What's left of her hair
Spears out in green and orange spikes;
Her eyes, a snowman's anthracite,
Look upon us with a stare
So hard we're forced to think that she dislikes
The lot of us, eager to fight
                With nail and tooth
Our flabby images of untruth.

           Her furious tattoos,
Those Jolly Rogers and daggered hearts,
Bleeding roses and poison darts,
Her fingernails in various hues
                Of pretended harlotry,
Are manifestos meant to address
And put to exquisite duress
                Her misguided family.

She's punctured her head with painful holes
In fervid hopes to shock our souls,
And yet she looks merely as grubby
As some punk baroness and her hubby
                At Epsom Downs or Ascot.
Cousin Lena's proud ambition
Was to shame us of our condition,
But there she sits, our cute mascot.

Listener

Uncle Duncan listens so intently
Your words inspect themselves with minute care.
Echoes, entendres, overtones multiply;
You hear suggestions that were never there
Until you opened to his expectant stare.

You fidget and begin to tell him things
You swore you'd never tell another living soul;
His patient impassivity still brings
More out, and more, until you've told it all.

And feel the better for it? No, not at all.
You feel you've been deceived in some dim way,
By some elusive seduction of your will.
You had to say the things you had to say
And now you wish you hadn't. And ever shall.

The Look

It's impossible there could be
Any conceivable complicity
Between you and Cousin Mary Rose.

Why then does she gaze at you
With a look that must imply
She knows you know she surely knows?

Her briefest glance has the quality
Of chilling perspicuity,
Discovering all your sexual woes,

Your tight financial anxiety,
Your marital infidelity—
All the secrets you'd never disclose

To another breathing entity.
But her knowingness is merely a pose
That lends importance to Mary Rose,
Because she *couldn't* know . . . Could she?

A Victim

His knees are wobbly, his face is gray,
His eyes bloodshot; a racking cough
Sounds liable to carry him off;
His stare is vacant, as if he may
Be unaccustomed to the light of day.

His mind is ruined, his form is wasted,
Who hours ago was hale and whole.
But Cousin Oliver (poor soul!)
Has tasted—mind you now, has barely tasted—
Aunt Lavinia's casserole.

Small World

Aunt Mae and Uncle Don have been
Married for fifty (my God!) years.
No one recalls when they began
To look like one another from ears
To ankles, the way some couples do
As decades intertwine their tastes
And distastes, hopes, and tacit fears.
Their features blur and soften, their waists
Thicken simultaneously,
Their eyesights fail together; she
Can't see what Uncle Don can't see.

And these resemblances don't end
With spouse and spouse. They seem to blend,
This childless duo, into their near
Environments, so that their house,
Their dog, their cat, their ancient car
Take on aspects of their face
And form. So long they've been together
That they comprise a private weather
That transforms all into a gray
And muted landscape unbrightened by
One odd or colorful detail,
Where every day's another day
Arriving, departing without fail
Under a low and motionless sky.

They're all alone together, we say,
But is it true? Presences
May range about them invisibly
To us; dim silent entities
Of dark desire and long remorse
May haunt their twilight universe
Of sweet or bitter memories
That time has worm almost away . . .

But that's at best a vague surmise.
In the noisy parlor they sit near—
She on the sofa, he in a chair—
And while we wonder why they're here,
Perhaps they wonder if we're there.

Photographer

She flies from set to set, from face
    To face. "Say cheese!" she cries
And flashes her bulbs at startled eyes
That go bright blind for a little space.

"Gotcha!" she crows. We all complain
    We were not ready. She flutters
Away, snapping her gum and shutters
At open-mouthed victims again and again.

The camera never lies, she avows;
    Its images are true:
Aunt Marjorie has red eyes, big blue
Ears, and gaping holes for a nose.

And Uncle Einar's wildly cross-eyed,
    And Uncle John's so dim
We'll always wonder if that's really him
Or a victim of subarctic frostbite.

Myself I won't describe except
    To say I hope to God
I don't look anything like so odd,
With my eyes closed as if I slept

In deeply stupid unconsciousness.
    She makes us look as scary
As old woodcuts in a bestiary—
But maybe, after all, that's us.

Slow Dance with Cousin Bradford

Silent, languid, almost somnolent,
He sits apart. His eyes half closed, he sways
Like a slender plume of steam rubbed by a hint
Of lazy breeze. He might sit like that for days.

He hears in his mind a delicate andante
That every graceful hour possesses him more:
The second movement of the Sinfonia Concertante
In E flat major, K. 364.

A Castle in Spain

Elizabeth's father outlines his complex scheme
To Uncle Einar, hoping he'll invest
A parcel of his vaunted capital
To help support his in-law's stardust dream.

The great man drops his head upon his chest,
Seeming to listen intently to it all.
Emboldened, he details it more and more,
Till silenced by the burr of Einar's snore.

Aunt Mary Recalls Her Mother's Advice

Her mother told her men are none too sharp;
     That's why women must wear
Bright colors three at a time, or four,
And swirl their tail fins like Japanese carp.

Alas, the male species is famous for
     Slow-wittedness. Alas, the male
Species anyhow. Let's have more
Colors—vermilion and gold, emerald and teal—

In skirt and scarf and blouse and belt and earring
     For thousands and thousands of years
And see if men can learn to name the hues.
And maybe Nature can improve their hearing

If women lend their cunning tender aid.
     Sing out, sweet ladies, in tones
So dulcet, so seductive they must move stones!
(*I.e.,* men.) That's what Mary's mother said.

Clotheshorse

But Cousin Tina has a dissenting thought,
    Although she dresses as modishly
As any twentysomething starlet who's been taught
What to wear to the flashbulb-bright soirée,
    Whom to schmooze and what to say.

The difference is that Tina's expensive strapless
      Is not designed
      To plant herself in mind.
She wriggles it on, childlike, hapless,
To make an impression she can hide behind.

Her whitened smile and daring décolleté
    And creamy shoulders are on display
      For everyone to see,
        But are not she.
She only exhibits this sexy array
To hide her bashful modesty.
And since menfolk are predictable jerks—

    It works.

It's a Gift

Whatever Cousin Hatfield thinks to do gets done.
To sue a corporation and destroy its power
      Requires the concentration of an hour;
            Then, if you'll spare a minute,
He'll teach you Philosophy and everything that's in it—
      And all accomplished in a spirit of fun.

      That's not exactly accurate:
      He works his miracles with such an air
Of easy grace, it's obvious he doesn't care
      That he might fail and look a fool
To the grubby rest of us who inch along by rule
      Of dusty rule books that we hate.
      We fear his secret fun may be to jeer
From smiling Olympus on us huddled masses here.

      Perhaps he's one of us inside.
      Perhaps a grievous error crumbles his pride
Or a hidden sorrow gnaws him bit by bit.
      Perhaps. I wouldn't count on it.

Common Knowledge

Uncle Lewis toils from set to set,
    From chair to chair,
Following the track of Aunt Nanette,
    Soothing feelings here and there,
Begging us please to forgive, please to forget.

She might be one whom the word *harridan*
    Was invented for,
Avid to insult woman and man
    With words like "sot" and "dirty whore."
She threatens each of us time and again.

But no one pays attention, for we all know
    What Uncle did
That January night so long ago,
    The thing he thought forever hid
That made her mind a waste of polar snow.

Mum's the Word

Aunt Melissa sits and sits
  And knits.
Uncle Charlie thinks and thinks
  And winks.
If I tell what's passed between
  The knitter and the thinker
It would undeniably mean
  That I'm a stinker.

The Traitor

He sits apart,
The watcher weaving his cramped designs,
Writing in sharp lines
Portraits of a family
Who furnish, endlessly,
Matter for which he has small heart.

Is it true that he betrays
Those whom he is obliged
To love if possible, to respect,
In any case?
And do they feel besieged,
Preferring cold neglect
To the ambivalent phrase
And unfair adjective
That slander the ways they live?

We all have faults,
So what? What need to point them out
With yellow mechanical pencil
Limning in simple stencil
Lines that fleer and pout
With crossgrain mockery that never halts?

His answer you'll intuit:
"Of this please have no doubt:
Someone's going to do it."

Dozing

Grandfather Settle dozes, aware
And unaware. The buzz and stutter,
Rasp and rattle of family
Mount and subside, a restless sea
Of signaling like the mutter
Of radiation from a darkened star.

He now inhabits a calmer space,
And nobler, than his kinfolk do.
If he regards them, it's from the distance
Half-sleep projects with mild persistence
Between all figures that come and go,
Casting dull shadows across his face.

The vivid continent unmoors
And drifts away, bearing its plains
And plaintive peoples eastward. Alone,
He has become an isle of stone
And coral, voices and light strains
Of music, shadows and undulant flowers.

Now, as the world withdraws its heat,
Unsteady pulse, and heartsickness
Farther and farther away, regret
Troubles him never. He may forget
The past or recall it as it was—
Even the parts that were incomplete.

It makes no difference.
                    Goodbye,
Nation of heedless ghosts. Farewell.
Grandfather Settles bids you peace
And happiness, prosperities
Beyond all count.
                    The whelming swell
Of flood tide divides the sky.

Grandfather

Eight times when the hour is eight,
He will punctually insist,
As a predictable fatalist,
We must meet our appointed fate;
But his sentence stands alone
When the hour is only one.
When the time is dead midnight
With its appalling lack of light,
He chokes our spirits with black gloom,
Intoning twelve times: *"Doom Doom Doom . . . "*

Aunt Wilma Reveals Her Cunning Design

Time was, I couldn't sleep. Peroxide floozies
Drifted about my brain, those tarts that Einar
Spent his substance on, deserting the finer
Things in life for What's-her-name and Whoozis.
What would happen if one entrapped my man,
Enticed the idiot to run away?
It's always smart to build a secret plan,
Lay by a nest egg for a rainy day.

And so I started to keep a calendar,
A kind of journal, listing all the dates and names
That he called Conquests and that I called Shames.
"I know who you're with and what you are;
Spare me your lies and that false sheepish grin.
You'll discover there's sweet hell to pay."
The good Lord knows, it's because of sneaking men
We need that nest egg for a rainy day.

So here's the cute arrangement that we made:
Whatever Einar spent on his taste of spice,
The same amount was doubled for my price,
And I had means of making sure he paid.
—You've called me mercenary, but, once again,
You'd be wise to listen to what I say
And think about the years come over us, Fran,
And of a nest egg for a rainy day.

Time passes swifter than the meteor
Slashing through the satin of the dark,
Swifter than a hearthfire's glancing spark
Burning all it is to be no more;
And I know well enough I've lost the face
To attract the eyes of suitors, my hair gone gray,
Crow's-feet crinkling my temples, my only grace
My little nest egg for a rainy day.

But a situation finds its remedy:
There'll come a certain hour when Einar's gone
To lie in earth a jolly skeleton
With no blond chippie perched on his bony knee,
And I'll give cash and coupons good employ;
I'll buy myself twelve outfits bright and gay
And buy myself a gorgeous expensive boy
To devour my nest egg all one rainy day.

The Strain of Mercy

Aunt Agnes takes it all in stride:
Uncle Einar's boorishness,
Cousin Lilias's need to hide,
Cousin Willoughby's sordid mess
He thinks is a "bohemian life,"
Aunt Alicia's wandering wits,
What Uncle Lewis did to his wife,
The way that Uncle Nahum sits
In his creepy corner and calculates,
Aunt Wilma's plans for sweet revenge,
Cousin Hubert in dire straits,
The inevitable and dreaded change
Coming to young Elizabeth,
Cousin Ellie's hordes of mates,
Uncle Ozzie's fear of death.

She recognizes what we are,
Yet holds us in affection
As steadfast as the morning star,
As if our faults had no connection
With the persons we are within.
She doesn't pretend an ignorance
Of our dark collective sin;
She only believes that circumstance
Has gone against us every one,
That by blind forces we were driven.

We make a painful silent moan
At being so horribly forgiven.

Elizabeth in the Porch Swing

The voices now grow quieter inside
As the clock strikes midnight. Elizabeth
Is sleeping fitfully within the wide
Dark porch past which the constellations glide
As slow as autumn's coming and as smooth.

Her vexed dreams undulate under a stream
Of murmurs that she hears and doesn't hear,
Purling from the grown-ups. There is one dream
That leaps and dances like a candleflame
And tells her clearly that she must beware.

Beware of what?—It's part of the deceit
Of dreams that they can make us shake with dread
And startle awake drenched in icy sweat,
Shivered from our topknots to our feet,
And sit up wide-eyed in the clammy bed.

There's more to dreams than we can wish to know.
Elizabeth is dreaming gibberish—and yet
She feels that what she dreams is truly so:
She's there inside her dream; its rainbow flow
Means much, though she can't say exactly what.

Perhaps she's changing into one of *them,*
A frowsy grown-up full of sound advice,
Dull saws to mumble in a steady hum.
Thoughtless as bumblebees, they drone and fume,
Forever faithful to their dull clichés.

And then her dream gives in to a mockingbird
Somewhere in the dark as it displays
Its genius repertoire. Each note is heard
Within her dream, each changes to a word
That coolly comforts her with what it says:

"Sleep on, little one, lullay lullaby.
For, swifter than you can calculate, the sun
Tumbles its yellow beachball up the sky
And down once more, marking a day gone by
That kissed your life but will not come again.

"Fear not: The rising of the heedful moon
Signals that nighttime is not the end
Of light, of time. An elegant lagoon
Of space buoys your world up like a balloon.
Fear not, Elizabeth, I am your friend."